MW01201619

HOW TO PROPAGATE, GROW & CARE FOR ROSES

Old Fashioned Know How for Modern Day Growers

Compiled and Edited By Alan Bloom

HOW TO PROPAGATE, GROW & CARE FOR ROSES

First Edition January 2017

Published by Wild Blooming Press

Printed by Create Space, United States of America

TABLE OF CONTENTS

INTRODUCTION

Roses truly are the most stunning of flowers. But when it comes to growing they can be quite tricky. This book uses good old fashioned know-how and makes the growing of roses easy-peasy.

It covers all the important details, great for the beginner and it also includes tips that the experts may not know…

Careful Preparation

Situation and Soils

Propagating Roses From Seed

Planting

Subsequent Treatment

Pruning

Manures

Growing Roses From Cuttings

Growing Roses on Barren Soil

Budding

Growing Roses for Show Blooms

All the above are covered in detail, including some lovely colour photographs of beautiful roses.

I hope you enjoy reading and learning more about these fascinating, stunning flowers.

Careful Preparation

Although, owing to the varying character of different buds, stocks, soil, climatic, and other conditions, it is impossible to lay down hard and fast rules for the guidance of those who desire to become growers of roses, whether in a large or a small way, experience has revealed that certain definite provision may be regarded as being indispensable to success.

In the first place it is necessary properly to appreciate the fact that, generally speaking, when a rose is planted it is intended to remain in that position for a considerable time; probably many years. Seeing that the rose is a fairly gross feeder, the fact immediately becomes apparent that, to secure the best results for over the longest period, it is essential to place at the disposal of the plants a substantial supply of suitable food.

Where limestone, rubble, and other unfavourable subsoils prevail, they must be removed and replaced with good loam, plentifully fortified with cow dung, old bones, and so on.

It has been discovered that all kinds of roses will not produce first class results in the same kind of soil. For example, the invaluable tea roses thrive and flower most profusely when grown in well drained, deep, highly fertile light soils, while hybrid teas and hybrid perpetuals do best, and produce blooms of the greatest substance, when accommodated in deep, rich, strong loams.

With those facts kept prominently in mind and studied and provided for, if circumstances will permit, the preparation of the ground may be proceeded with. This will entail some solid graft, but don't shirk the job. Remember that every ounce of extra labour, well directed, will represent so much more capital and a relatively higher rate of interest in the way of blooms in the years to come.

Situation and Soils

Roses are best planted in a position, if possible, that is sheltered from strong north and westerly winds, but not too near trees or hedges. Positions open to the east or south are best, provided they are situated so as to afford plenty of sunlight.

To provide protection from prevailing winds a fence or trellis upon which climbing roses can be grown is recommended.

As frosts are seldom so severe in this climate as to prove inurious to a rose, with rare exceptions, it isn't a big concern.

The best soil for roses is undoubtedly a rich deep tenacious loam, but not actual clay. Where the soil is the reverse to this, that is light, sandy and shallow, some heavy loam or clay should be obtained and worked into the natural soil, failing this the difficulty of obtaining good roses will be greatly increased, involving the use of much heavy manure, and a largely augmented water supply. Still good roses can be, and are produced on comparatively light soils.

If it is desired to grow roses in perfection, they should be allotted a separate bed or portion of the garden. Should this be low and not naturally drained, this must be artificially provided. Trenches 2 feet 6 inches to 3 feet deep and 25 to 30 feet apart with a fall of about 1 feet in 25, should be dug, and along the bottom of these ordinary field drain pipes are laid and covered with brushwood or any similar available material, the trenches are then filled in. The general effect of such drainage is to greatly improve the soil, rendering it more open and less liable to bake and crack during periods of drought, while even a light soil will retain moisture for a longer period than would a similar soil undrained. It is, of course, imperative that all soils, no matter what their nature or position, should be well trenched to a depth of 18 inches or 2 feet, a liberal supply of manure being at the same time dug in. Manure from a dairy-farm yard being best for light soils, while ordinary stable manure is more suited to a heavy or clay soil.

Propagating Roses From Seed

Choose your parent blooms while they are only half open, before the stamens show.

Cut the male parent flower and put it in water in the house, away from bees; and then take a sharp knife and a square of butter muslin to the bud which is to be the female parent.

The stamens must not be showing.

Remove the central petals and cut away every stamen, leaving the stigma untouched and unharmed; and cover it then, with the butter muslin.

When, within a few hours, the stigma becomes sticky and the pollen on the male bloom inside the house becomes floury and adheres easily to your finger, take the cut bloom to the female flower and lightly touch the pollen-laden anthers to the stigma.

The pollen should adhere easily and your first job is ended; replace the butter muslin and leave it there for three or four days.

If your fertilisation was effective, the seed pod will begin to swell within a week or so – and then you wait for the seed to ripen. Roses may take eight months to ripen.

Most seed, other than roses, should be held until the next normal planting season, but rose seed, ripening normally in July, should be planted immediately – and you can expect the first young blooming in November.

Planting

The ground being ready, the positions for our plants can be marked off. These should be 4 feet apart, or a somewhat smaller distance may be allowed in the case of the less vigorous tea roses.

As some sort of support will in many cases be necessary, it is best to procure some hardwood stakes, 5 feet long and 1 and a quarter inches square, pointed at one end and driven into the ground sufficiently to render them secure. Near to these holes may be dug 12 to 15 inches square and sufficiently deep to enable us to bring the bud – if a budded rose – below the surface of the soil, so that in time roots will be thrown off from the bud as well as the stock upon which they are first worked.

It will, of course, be understood that we are here dealing with stocks which have not been worked at a greater height than 18 inches from the root base.

Those budded at a greater height cannot be safely brought low enough to allow the budded portion of the plant to take root.

Before actually planting our roses it will be well to examine them as to their condition upon arrival from the grower.

Once done, they may then be finally planted, taking care to spread out the roots so as to allow the soil to be well distributed among and around them.

Next fill up the holes completely, and tead firmly around the plants and finish off by leaving a complete ring or mound of soil two or three inches high and twelve inches from the stems. This basin may be mulched or filled up with well decomposed stable manure and watered at once, so as to completely settle and moisten the surrounding soil.

In this connection it may be well to point out that no manure should be allowed to come in actual contact with the roots of newly planted roses. It may and should be liberally used in the preparation of the ground, and in surface dressings, both at planting and subsequently, but if thrown into the holds in the process of filling up, the plants are sure to be retarded rather than benefited, or they may be killed outright.

It will prove advantageous in hot and dry districts to protect the newly planted roses from wind and sun by means of leafy branches of trees or shrubs stuck in the ground around and near them until they appear to be established.

They should also receive occasional waterings, say at fortnightly intervals, if the weather proves to be dry after planting.

And it is well to bear in mind that a good soaking at longer intervals is much better for the plants than oft repeated surface sprinklings.

In the matter of arrangement of the several groups into which roses are usually divided, it is, of course, wise to keep separate tea, or truly perpetual blooming roses, from hybrid perpetual, or more particularly spring flowering varieties, while climbers belonging to both groups should preferably be grown on a trellis apart from dwarf varieties.

Much will, of course, depend upon the resources of individual growers.

Roses planted in beds should all be named, particularly when grown for exhibition purposes. My practice is to name all our plants in a permanent manner by writing the name boldly with a soft lead pencil on a piece of planed Oregon or deal 20 inches long by 1 and a half wide, covered with paint or white lead. These labels are driven into the ground in front of and some little distance from the plants. Another good plan is to attach the name on a smaller piece of wood to the support stakes.

Subsequent Treatment

Under this heading we propose to deal with some of the more important points in the further growth and management of newly planted roses. We have assumed the plants, as received from the nursery, were pruned, although this is not usually the case for nursery stock seldom do more than shorten back the principal shoots, many of their customers preferring to exercise their own judgment as to the mode and extent of pruning.

For the first year, or even more, it will be necessary to encourage the growth and development of the plants to the fullest extent, even at the expense of some of the earlier blooms.

Therefore, throughout the first season the ground should be kept clear of weeds by occasional dutch-hoeings. And growth encouraged by copious watering during dry weather, and towards the end of summer one or two waterings with liquid manure will prove beneficial.

No further solid stimulus will be required for the first year other than the mulching at the time of planting, assuming the ground to have been properly trenched and manured at the outset.

The plants will doubtless bloom freely during autumn, but the formation of strong shoots well furnished with foliage and buds is of greater importance just now, and should be encouraged even at the expense of the former, our aim being to secure plants furnished with well matured growths before mid-winter.

HOW TO PROPAGATE, GROW & CARE FOR ROSES

Pruning

Nearly everyone who has attempted to grow roses recognises the necessity for pruning of some kind. There is a right and wrong method of procedure in this, as in nearly every operation connected with horticulture.

It must be borne in mind that a rose is not a tree to grow outwards and upwards continuously, but from year to year forms fresh channels in the way of new and vigorous shoots for the flow of the sap, consequently the supply to the older growths becomes diminished, hence the necessity for their removal.

The objects of pruning then should be – to maintain a well balanced supply of sap – the life and strength of the rose – throughout the plants, to mould and preserve their shape, and to ensure vigour, colour, and substance to their blooms.

The pruning of plants which have been well grown and carefully pruned at the outset is a comparatively easy matter; unfortunately a large proportion of the roses commonly sold are not well grown, and not infrequently a full year or more may be thrown away in the endeavour to recover lost ground, so that plants which at first appeared a bargain may prove very dear in the long run.

The golden rule as applied to pruning is, that the stronger a plant or shoot the greater the number of buds to be left, and conversely, the weaker a plant or variety, the fewer its buds for future growths; the object being to increase the sap-flow to a limited number of buds, and thus ensure more vigorous shoots and blooms.

At first sight it may appear strange to a novice that a weakly plant should be almost exterminated, in order to secure its subsequent vigorous development.

It is, however, a truth every rose grower has repeatedly verified for himself. In the case of plants specially set apart for the production of show blooms the pruning should be even more severe than is the practice when it is merely a matter of a well formed plant grown for decorative purposes only.

During June, with certain reservations, all shoots should be rigorously cut back two or three eyes or buds, while it is not infrequently advisable to restrict the buds to one only in the case of certain weakly varieties, as the production of one vigorous growth is to be preferred to two or three spindley ones. All weak and worn out wood should be entirely removed in fact, everything which is likely to restrict the sap-supply of cherished shoots or blooms should be ruthlessly cut away.

Some experience in the habits and mode of growth of certain varieties is necessary to enable us to know which shoots to retain and which to remove.

HOW TO PROPAGATE, GROW & CARE FOR ROSES

Manures

The question of the application is an important one, and as it arises, in so far as its application in the solid form is concerned, shortly after the pruning season, we propose to deal with it in accordance with our own usage, though this may be at variance, to some extent, with the practice of other successful growers.

First, after pruning and cleaning our rose beds, we invariably apply a good dressing of well decomposed cow manure which has been occasionally turned, and so sweetened and made ready for assimilation when incorporated with the soil.

This is lightly dug in over the entire surface of the beds, care being taken to avoid injury to the roots of the plants.

In addition to this winter dressing, we at a later stage apply a surface mulching of lighter manure, generally ordinary stable manure which has lain for a time.

This, besides being in itself beneficial, prevents undue evaporation and ensures a more complete absorption of any water or liquid manure applied to the beds during the summer months.

Another, and perhaps the best, mode for the application of manure, is in the liquid form. This can be given at any time, and being fluid is in the best condition for immediate assimilation; for necessarily all plants absorb nutriment in a fluid condition only.

Moreover, it can always be given without in any way disturbing the roots, and can of course be with-held when and where not needed, which is not always the case when dealing with rose beds during winter.

One of the safest liquid manures is made by filing a 28 pound bag with fresh cow manure, adding 2 pounds of soot and soaking in 25 gallons of water for a week; give each plant, say, half a gallon.

This should preferably be given after rain or a soaking with clean water. It is particularly serviceable just before and during the expansion of the blooms, and again in autumn, prior to the later or autumnal blooming period. Cesspool liquid and drainage from cow sheds and stables, when available, are undoubtedly most beneficial.

Various artificial and chemical manures can be used with advantage. Among the best of these are sulphate of ammonia and nitrate of soda, also various guanos, both natural and artificial.

An effective chemical manure for use on established plants can be made as follows:- 1 ounce nitrate of potash, 1 ounce of phosphate of potash, in 1 and a half gallons of water.

In ground which is deficient in lime or chalk, a beneficial result will be attained by giving a light surface dressing of slacked lime, forking same well in during winter.

In ground which is deficient in lime or chalk, a beneficial result will be attained by giving a light surface dressing of slacked lime, forking same well in during winter.

Growing Roses From Cuttings

There are different aspects to take into consideration when taking rose cuttings:-

1. Choose wood from strong, vigorous growing roses only (including all climbing roses).
2. Use ripened wood of the past season's growth only, not old wood and not immature wood.
3. Take the cutting with a heel, if possible. The sap supply is heaviest at the junction of a young branch where it grows out from an older branch.
4. Make cuttings 6 to 8 inches long. Use a sharp knife and trim the heel clean from splinters and tearing.
5. In hot areas suffering from drought, make cuttings ready for planting, then immerse in a basin of water for 24 hours. Plant immediately afterwards.

Have a small patch dug over in readiness for the cuttings. Open a drill (or ditch) about 4 or 5 inches deep along the line of planting.

Flood the open drill with water.

Place the cuttings upright in the open row, half in, half out, of the drill, 6 inches apart.

Turn back soil with rake to surface level, then firm the soil well against cuttings on each side.

Use your boots, one foot on each side of the cutting, and firm the soil with all your weight.

Then rake surface soil loose and level, and leave tidy.

Growing Roses on Barren Soil

Many lovers of flowers would like to grow a few roses to beautify their homes, but are prevented from attempting to do so by reason of barren soil being available.

Now, almost any kind of soil can be made to grow roses, and good roses, by taking some pains and preparing it properly before planting.

Roses like a somewhat stiff soil with a little clay in it, and the very poorest of soil can be made good enough for these beautiful flowers by the method described below.

The soil should be trenched to a depth of 2 feet, and in the bottom of each trench 6 inches of good coarse stockyard or stable manure should be placed.

Then fill in 6 inches, of soil, and on top of this another layer of manure 6 inches deep. Six inches more of the soil can then be added, and on top of this a layer of well rotted manure, or vegetable mould if procurable.

Then fill in the rest of the soil, and allow it to lie for a month or so before planting.

When planting the roses, work a handful of blood and bone into the bottom of each hole, set the plants firmly in the ground, water well if the soil is dry, and then mulch each plant with 3 inches, of course manure.

If it is too much of an undertaking to trench the whole of the garden in this way, holes may be dug out where each rose is to go, and filled in exactly the same manner. The most unpromising soils treated in this way will grow excellent roses, and the trouble and labour expended will be well repaid by the profusion of beautiful blooms which the plants will yield during the summer.

Budding

Rose budding is quite a simple operation. In budding, the first operation is to prepare the stock. If this is an unbudded briar, two or three side briar shoots should have been left earlier in the season, and have made by now good shoots about the thickness of a pencil.

Strip the leaves from the base of these, near their junction with the old woods, and at the same time rub off any thorns. Do this a few days before budding, as it will give any wounds made a chance to heal.

In the case of roses already budded and which it is proposed to rebud, cut off all growth, leaving from three to six shoots of young wood of pencil thickness as near the main stem as possible, and trimming off the leaves as in the case of briars.

The young shoots must not be too sappy, or they will snap off during the operation.

Having prepared the shoots, it would be as ell to deluge each plant with water, as a free flow of sap is necessary to ensure success.

For very old roses a little sulphate of ammonia added to the water will be of great advantage and cause a freer and quicker flow of sap.

<u>Selecting the Buds</u>

The stocks prepared, next procure the buds to be inserted. The best buds, and the quickest to start into growth, will be found on a flowering stem from which the old flower has just dropped off. Cut this off and with a sharp knife trim off all the leaves, leaving a piece of leaf stem half an inch long attached.

The most suitable buds are those growing on the middle of the shoot. These will have commenced to swell, but have not yet come into leaf.

Inserted into a free flowing sap they will set and commence growth at once. Buds taken from near the base of a shoot are often apt to remain dormant in the autumn and only start into growth the following spring.

The Actual Operation

When everything is in readiness make an incision with a keen-edged knife across the shoot and as near to the base as possible; make it just below a leaf, cutting through the bark, but not into the wood.

Then make a second cut downwards from the first, so as to form a T-shaped scar. Raise the edges of the bark gently with the point of the knife.

In cutting the bud insert the knife half an inch below the bud, and with a cut upwards take off a thin shield-like piece of bark; with the leaf stalk and the bud it contains and a thin piece of wood attached.

Hold the cut upwards by its upper end between the thumb and forefinger, and with the knife gently raise the wood from the bark and wrench it out.

The piece of wood must come out clean. If difficult to get away it is a sign that the buds are hardly sappy enough, and should be placed in water for an hour or more to render them freer.

Care must also be taken that the bud itself is not snapped out whilst removing the wood. The bud safely removed, insert the bottom of it in the opening of the T-shaped slit, and with the aid of the piece of leaf stalk push it down to the bottom of the slit. What bark remains outside should be cut off even with the crosscut, and the edges pressed over the bud as closely as possible.

Then tie the whole firmly with a ligature of raffia, candle cotton, or some other soft material. The shoots can be curtailed a little, but on no account cut them back close to the bud.

Subsequent Treatment

After a few days the ties can be loosened, and in a fortnight's time they can be removed entirely. Then head the stock back further to encourage growth in the bud. As soon as the bud commences to make rapid growth pinch the top out, and so induce a sturdy side growth. The long single shoot may, if left, be blown out by the wind. After nipping, head the stock back to within 3 inches of the bud and encourage rapid growth with an abundance of water. In a few weeks a fine large new rose in full bloom will be produced.

HOW TO PROPAGATE, GROW & CARE FOR ROSES

Growing Roses for Show Blooms

Do not allow your roses to become crowded with too much growth. Rub off the inner buds of the rose that will not have room to mature and keep the roses open in the centre.

Watch for insect and scale pests on your roses, and treat at once to prevent multiplying.

Keep your rose beds well hoed, as it keeps the soil open, and saves watering often, and acts as a mulch. It keeps the plants growing, and keeps plant enemies moving.

Disbudding, and selecting the required buds and liquid manuring are all necessary for success on the show benches.

Show roses should be true to colour, free from blemishes, high pointed, well-formed buds, just bursting, and must not have broken or double centres.

The bottom rose petals should never be removed and should not be too large or coarse.

THE END

References

1945 'GROWING ROSES FROM CUTTINGS', *The Argus (Melbourne, Vic. : 1848 - 1957)*, 11 May, p. 8. , viewed 23 Jan 2017, http://nla.gov.au/nla.news-article1095579

1901 'GROWING ROSES.', *West Gippsland Gazette (Warragul, Vic. : 1898 - 1930)* , 10 September, p. 4. (MORNING.), viewed 23 Jan 2017, http://nla.gov.au/nla.news-article68705043

1898 'Growing Roses on Barren Soil.', *The Queenslander (Brisbane, Qld. : 1866 - 1939)*, 22 October, p. 806. (Unknown), viewed 24 Jan 2017, http://nla.gov.au/nla.news-article20852643

1912 'SEASONABLE GARDENING NOTES', *The Express and Telegraph (Adelaide, SA : 1867 - 1922)*, 16 November, p. 5. (FRIDAY'S EDITION.), viewed 24 Jan 2017, http://nla.gov.au/nla.news-article209966535

1924 'Growing Roses for Show Blooms', *The Daily Mail (Brisbane, Qld. : 1903 - 1926)*, 24 August, p. 16. , viewed 24 Jan 2017, http://nla.gov.au/nla.news-article219443596

1919 'THE FLORAL REALM.', *The Journal (Adelaide, SA : 1912 - 1923)*, 3 May, p. 17. (NIGHT EDITION), viewed 24 Jan 2017, http://nla.gov.au/nla.news-article204711291

1950 'Try growing your roses from seed', *Truth (Sydney, NSW : 1894 - 1954)*, 10 December, p. 34. , viewed 24 Jan 2017, http://nla.gov.au/nla.news-article167981601

Printed in the USA
CPSIA information can be obtained
at www.ICGtesting.com
LVHW081131011023
759816LV00001B/8

* 9 7 8 1 5 4 2 7 3 6 8 7 9 *